THE
Jewish Mourner's
HANDBOOK

THE
Jewish Mourner's
HANDBOOK

BEHRMAN HOUSE

PHOTOGRAPHIC CREDITS

Photographs supplied by Quicksilver Photographers, Washington, D.C., Smithsonian Traveling Exhibition Service

Burial Society, Mikulov and Jewish Museum, Mikulov (Nikolsburg), Moravia (Front Cover).
State Museum in Prague
Cycle of Burial Society Paintings Prague, ca. 1780
(Pages 12, 15, 16, 18, 20, 27, 30, 33, 34, 36, 53).
These paintings depicting the activities of the Prague Burial Society originally hung in the meeting room where members gathered for their annual banquet. A date of ca. 1780 is suggested by developments in the community at that time. The reforms of Joseph II began at this time and threatened many Jewish customs and organizations. The Prague cycle, with its emphasis on charitable acts and on the importance of the burial society within the Jewish community, may have been commissioned by the Society to assert its position in the face of these reforms.

TRANSLATION CREDITS
Translations of Psalm 23 and Psalm 121 by Rabbi David Polish.
The Publisher thanks the Central Conference of American Rabbis for permission to reproduce these translations.

PROJECT EDITOR: TERRY KAYE

BOOK DESIGN: BARBARA HUNTLEY

COVER PHOTO: BURIAL SOCIETY PITCHER
JEWISH MUSEUM, MIKULOV, MORAVIA

COPYRIGHT © 1992 BEHRMAN HOUSE, INC.
235 WATCHUNG AVENUE, WEST ORANGE, NJ 07052
ISBN 0-87441-528-4

MANUFACTURED IN THE UNITED STATES OF AMERICA

EDITORIAL COMMITTEE

CHAIRMAN: RABBI WILLIAM CUTTER

RABBI LEE T. BYCEL

GEORGIANNE FISHER CUTTER, M.S.W.

DR. ELLIOT DORFF

BENJAMIN DWOSKIN, M.A.

RABBI ADAM FISHER

RABBI RALPH P. KINGSLEY

DR. DAVID KRAEMER

RABBI HAROLD KRAVITZ

DR. JOSEPH LUKINSKY

RABBI JEHIEL ORENSTEIN

RABBI DAVID POLISH

CYNTHIA REICH, M.A., M.S.

RABBI SANDY EISENBERG SASSO

CANTOR WILLIAM SHARLIN

DR. DAVID A. TEUTSCH

LINDA THAL, B.A.

CONTENTS

"Our days are like grass;

we bloom like the flower of the field;

a wind passes by and it is no more."

Psalm 103:15-16

PREFACE

JUDAISM embraces all of life and accepts death as a part of life. At the same time, Jewish tradition understands that we are never prepared to lose someone we love. In the face of death we are confronted by powerful emotions and questions to which we have no answers. That is when ritual shows its greatest strength. Judaism presents us with a highly structured series of procedures that can help us through our grief and ease us back into the rhythm of life. Jewish tradition recognizes our confused emotions and shows us how to act on them in clearly demarcated stages of mourning.

There is comfort and security in the knowledge that centuries of tradition lie behind each of these practices, as we do what our parents did before us and their parents before them.

A Special House for Preparing the Body for Burial
Johann Christoph Bodenschatzen 1748

"One generation goes, another comes,
but the world remains forever."

Ecclesiastes 1:4

WHEN DOES THE FUNERAL TAKE PLACE?

THE funeral and burial are held as soon after death as possible. Judaism considers it a dishonor to the deceased to delay burial unnecessarily. In addition, prolonging the burial subjects the bereaved to even greater strain and despair. Usually the funeral is held early in the day. The exact timing, of course, depends on the availability of the funeral home and the schedule of the rabbi, who should be contacted before the time is set.

There are instances in which the funeral can be delayed. Funerals are not held at the following times: on Shabbat; on the Festival Days of Pesach, Shavuot and Sukkot; or on the High Holy Days. In special circumstances or when family and friends have to travel great distances to attend the funeral, a postponement is certainly acceptable.

"When I cry out in the night before You,
let my prayer reach You;
incline Your ear to my cry."

Psalm 88:2-3

WHAT IS AN ONEN?

UPON the death of a loved one, until the time of burial, each immediate relative (parent, spouse, child or sibling) is referred to as an *onen* (fem. *onenet*). Although in a state of shock and distress, the *onen* is occupied with the immediacy of practical arrangements. Some of these arrangements will require the advice and aid of your rabbi, the funeral home, and even hospital personnel.

Family and friends must be notified of the death. The *onen* usually does not receive condolence calls. The family of the deceased is allowed the privacy of grief. Close friends, however, may offer to help with the funeral arrangements.

Carrying the Body from the House
Prague ca. 1780

Because the mitzvah of caring for the dead is so important, the *onen* is freed of certain ritual obligations. For example, the *onen* need not pray, recite blessings or put on tefillin. On Shabbat, however, many of the laws that pertain to the *onen* fall away. Shabbat observances are performed and synagogue services attended. Your rabbi should be consulted for more detailed information.

Making the Coffin
Prague ca. 1780

"The dust returns to the earth as it was;
the spirit returns to God who gave it."

Ecclesiastes 12:7

WHAT KIND OF CASKET IS USED?

JUDAISM discourages ostentatious funerals. Loved ones are buried with simplicity and dignity. The traditional Jewish coffin is made of plain wood. It need not be lined or padded. Small holes are sometimes drilled in the bottom. The coffin may have metal handles or nails, although it is customary among traditional Jews to use wooden-pegged caskets. Sometimes a bag filled with earth from Israel is placed under the head, and some of the soil is sprinkled over the body. Usually no worldly possessions are placed in the coffin with the deceased, although the bereaved sometimes choose to put a small token of love into the casket.

Simplicity is always to be encouraged. In Israel, for example, the deceased is wrapped only in linens and is buried directly in the ground.　　Bodily remains are returned to the earth as quickly as possible ("For dust you are and to dust you shall return" - Genesis 3:19).

All branches of Judaism discourage the viewing of the body other than for proper identification.　　We are encouraged to remember our beloved ones in the vibrancy of their lives.

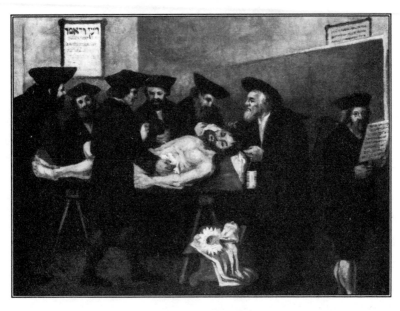

Washing the Body
Prague ca. 1780

"As we come forth, so shall we return."

Ecclesiastes 5:14

WHAT ARE THE PREPARATIONS BEFORE BURIAL?

BEFORE the body is buried, it is washed in a ritual act of purification called *taharah*. Just as a baby is washed and enters the world clean and pure, so do we leave the world cleansed by the religious act of *taharah*.

The cleansing is performed by the funeral director and staff, or the ritual of *taharah* may be carried out by the Ḥevra Kaddisha ("holy society"). The Ḥevra Kaddisha is a group of specially trained Jews who care for the body and prepare it for burial. Strict procedures are followed, which include the recitation of prayers and psalms. Men handle male bodies and women prepare female bodies; modesty is preserved even in death. Your rabbi may be consulted to find out if there is a Ḥevra Kaddisha in your area.

In traditional Jewish practice the deceased is not left alone from the time of death until burial. This ritual act of *shemirah* ("watching," "guarding") is performed as a sign of

Making the Shroud
Prague ca. 1780

respect to the deceased. A *shomer* ("watcher") may be hired to perform this service.

After the body is cleansed, it is dressed in shrouds (in Hebrew, *tachrichim*). The shrouds are simple and plain and made of white cotton or linen. Some people are buried in their typical daily dress. Men are buried with a tallit over the shroud or suit. Women are sometimes buried in a tallit if it was their practice to wear one when praying. One of the fringes of the tallit is cut to show that it will no longer be used.

"And Jacob rent his garments
and put on sackcloth,
and mourned for his son many days."

Genesis 37:34

WHAT IS KERIAH?

KERIAH is a Hebrew word meaning "tearing." It refers to the act of tearing one's clothes or cutting a black ribbon worn on one's clothes. This rending is a striking expression of grief and anger at the loss of a loved one.

Keriah is an ancient tradition. When our Patriarch Jacob believed his son Joseph was dead, he tore his garments (Genesis 37:34). Likewise, in II Samuel 1:11 we are told that King David and all the men with him took hold of their clothes and rent them upon hearing of the death of Saul and Jonathan. Job, too, in grieving for his children stood up and rent his clothes (Job 1:20).

Keriah is performed by the child, parent, spouse, and sibling of the deceased. It is usually done at the funeral home before the funeral service begins. If a black ribbon is used, it is provided by the funeral director. *Keriah* is

Keriah Ribbon

always performed standing. The act of standing shows strength at a time of grief. A cut is made on the left side of the clothing for parents - over the heart - and on the right side for all other relatives. Sometimes people choose to express deep feelings of grief by cutting on the left side for relatives other than their parents.

As the tear or cut is made, the family recites the following blessing:

בָּרוּךְ אַתָּה יְיָ אֱלֹהֵינוּ מֶלֶךְ הָעוֹלָם דַּיַּן הָאֱמֶת.

Baruch atah Adonai Eloheinu melech ha'olam dayan ha'emet.

Blessed are You, Adonai Our God, Ruler of the Universe, Judge of Truth.

The torn garment or ribbon is worn during the seven days of shiva (but not on Shabbat and Festival Days). Some people continue the practice for the thirty-day period of mourning.

PSALM 23

A Psalm of David

God is my shepherd, I shall not want.
God makes me lie down in green pastures,
Leads me beside still waters,
and restores my soul.
You lead me in right paths
for the sake of Your Name
Even when I walk in the valley of the
shadow of death
I shall fear no evil,
for You are with me;
Your rod and Your staff - they comfort me.
You have set a table before me in the presence
of my enemies;
You have anointed my head with oil;
my cup overflows.
Surely goodness and mercy shall follow me
all the days of my life,
And I shall dwell in the house of God forever.

"God leads me beside still waters."

Psalm 23:2

WHAT HAPPENS AT THE FUNERAL SERVICE?

JEWISH funerals are characterized by brevity and simplicity. They are designed for the honor and dignity of the deceased and are a part of the mourning process which helps comfort the bereaved.

In recent times, funerals have come to be held in funeral chapels. In the past the funeral service began in the home of the deceased. Psalms were recited, and a procession led the body to the burial-site. Today the larger portion of the funeral service takes place in the funeral chapel or synagogue. Sometimes the entire service is conducted at the gravesite.

The bereaved family is seated in the front row of the chapel or synagogue. The closed coffin remains in view. Traditionally, the coffin is not decorated with flowers. Instead of sending flowers in the name of the deceased, a donation can be made to charity.

The Eulogy
Prague ca. 1780

A brief introductory piece of music is sometimes played. This music is usually selected from the Jewish tradition and should be simple and not overly sentimental.

The service may begin with one or more psalms. The psalm most commonly recited is Psalm 23. The rabbi, cantor or leader of the service will then proceed with several readings from Psalms or other inspirational sources.

The eulogy is most often delivered by the rabbi, who has met with the family prior to the funeral to learn about the deceased and the particular attributes the family would like mentioned. The eulogy will typically contain personal reminiscences and sometimes humorous anecdotes as well. Often the family will write down special memories they have of the deceased which the rabbi then reads. The process of writing can help the family. They are comforted when their own words are read. The eulogy may also be delivered by a member of the family or a close friend.

The final prayer of the funeral service is the *El Malei Rahamim* (Hebrew for "God, full of compassion").

At the close of the service an announcement is made informing those present where and when the initial period of mourning will be observed.

EL MALEI RAHAMIM
Memorial Prayer

אֵל מָלֵא רַחֲמִים, שׁוֹכֵן בַּמְּרוֹמִים, הַמְצֵא מְנוּחָה
נְכוֹנָה תַּחַת כַּנְפֵי הַשְּׁכִינָה, בְּמַעֲלוֹת קְדוֹשִׁים
וּטְהוֹרִים כְּזֹהַר הָרָקִיעַ מַזְהִירִים, אֶת נִשְׁמַת...
שֶׁהָלַךְ לְעוֹלָמוֹ (שֶׁהָלְכָה לְעוֹלָמָה). בַּעֲבוּר שֶׁנָּדְרוּ
צְדָקָה בְּעַד הַזְכָּרַת נִשְׁמָתוֹ (נִשְׁמָתָה), בְּגַן עֵדֶן תְּהֵא
מְנוּחָתוֹ (מְנוּחָתָה). לָכֵן בַּעַל הָרַחֲמִים יַסְתִּירֵהוּ
(יַסְתִּירֶהָ) בְּסֵתֶר כְּנָפָיו לְעוֹלָמִים, וְיִצְרוֹר בִּצְרוֹר
הַחַיִּים אֶת נִשְׁמָתוֹ (נִשְׁמָתָה). יְיָ הוּא נַחֲלָתוֹ
(נַחֲלָתָה); וְיָנְוּחַ (וְתָנְוּחַ) עַל מִשְׁכָּבוֹ (מִשְׁכָּבָהּ)
בְּשָׁלוֹם, וְנֹאמַר אָמֵן.

Exalted God full of compassion, grant the fullness of
Your peace to the soul of .... who has gone to his
(her) eternal rest. May (s)he share in the glory of the
upright, the luster of whose purity is as the brightness
of the firmament. His (Her) memory lives in the
hearts of his (her) dear ones as an inspiration to deeds
of charity and goodness. May (s)he be granted the
bliss of eternal life. Shelter him (her) forever, merciful
God, under the wings of Your protecting love, and
may his (her) soul be bound up in the bond of eternal
life. God is his (her) possession. May (s)he rest
in peace. Amen.

Burial Procession Entrance into the Cemetery
Prague ca. 1780

"God has given, and God has taken away;
Blessed be the name of God."

Job 1:21

WHAT IS THE INTERMENT PROCEDURE?

AT the conclusion of the chapel service, family and friends who will attend the burial service form a procession behind the hearse and travel in convoy to the gravesite. Accompanying the dead is a mitzvah in the Jewish tradition.

At the burial site, the casket is removed from the hearse and carried by the pallbearers to the grave. The rabbi leads the procession. Usually at least six people are needed to carry the casket. It is considered a great honor to be a pallbearer. The Talmud illustrates the importance of the mitzvah when it says (Ketubbot 17a): "One must abandon the study of Torah to carry the dead [to their resting place]." The practice of family and friends carrying the deceased to the grave dates back to Biblical times when Jacob's sons carried him into the land of Canaan and buried him there (Genesis 50:13). It is also quite common for the coffin to be placed on a special cemetery wagon and wheeled to the gravesite.

As an indication of our reluctance to take leave of our loved one forever, the procession pauses several times on the way to the gravesite. Seven stops are traditional, but this number may vary.

During the procession Psalm 91 is recited. This beautiful psalm is also known as the "Song of the Spirit." It expresses confidence that God will watch over us.

Upon reaching the grave, a prayer called *Tzidduk Hadin* (Hebrew for "submission to Divine judgment") is often recited. *Tzidduk Hadin* acknowledges God's judgment and righteousness; it asks for God's mercy; and it accepts the inevitability of death as part of the Divine plan. *Tzidduk Hadin* is not recited when the somber theme of the prayer is incompatible with the spirit of certain holidays, such as Ḥannukah and Purim. Another prayer is then substituted.

The customs and practices surrounding the interment vary within each branch of Judaism. The coffin is lowered into the grave by hand or by mechanical device. The earth is shoveled onto the coffin. It is considered both a duty and an honor to help in filling the grave. As this is done, the shovel is usually not passed directly from one person to the next, but is placed on the ground before being picked up each time. This gesture symbolizes the hope that the tragedy of death will not pass from one person to another. It also symbolizes the desire not to rush this final parting from the deceased.

Digging the Grave
Prague ca. 1780

Some families prefer not to be present for the lowering of the coffin. They may wish to place several handfuls of earth on the coffin, which is then lowered after the mourners leave.

There is some variation in the final prayers recited at graveside. Sometimes the *El Malei Raḥamim* is said, sometimes Psalm 49. A special burial Kaddish may replace the Mourner's Kaddish.

Lowering the Coffin into the Grave
Prague ca. 1780

Upon leaving the cemetery, Jews traditionally form two lines and as the bereaved pass between them they recite the words: "May the Lord comfort you among the other mourners of Zion and Jerusalem" ("Ha'makom yenahem etchem betoch she'ar avelei Tzion vi'Yerushalayim"). This custom marks the family's transition into a state of formal mourning. The focus has changed from honoring the deceased to comforting the mourners.

Private rituals have developed over many years. For example, some Jews pull up a few blades of grass as they leave the cemetery. This was originally done as an expression of faith in resurrection. Just as the plucked grass would grow once more, so would we and our loved ones live again. Another explanation is that it is done to illustrate the transient nature of life.

Some wash their hands upon leaving the cemetery as a symbol of purification after being in contact with the dead. This may also be done upon entering the house of mourning.

Washing Hands on Leaving the Cemetery
Prague ca. 1780

"Let there be peace from heaven,
and life upon us and all Israel."

from the Mourner's Kaddish

WHAT IS KADDISH?

THE prayer we call Kaddish appears in every worship service. There are five variations of the basic Kaddish; one of them is the Mourner's Kaddish. This prayer is one of the most beautiful in Judaism, and many find its words a comfort when they are sorrowful. The cadences are important for the bereaved even when the meaning of specific words may not be known.

The Kaddish is an ancient prose-poem that developed over a period of centuries. Among its earlier purposes was to divide parts of the service. With the exception of the last verse, which is in Hebrew, the Kaddish is written in Aramaic, the language spoken by our people in the time of Ezra in the fifth century B.C.E. and for many centuries thereafter.

"Kaddish" is an Aramaic word meaning "sancti-fication." It is related to the Hebrew word *kadosh* ("holy").

Though most versions of the Kaddish contain no mention of death, the Kaddish came to be recited by mourners during the 13th century. It praises God, affirms God's holiness, and anticipates the establishment of peace on earth. At the very moment when our faith may be most tested, we praise God, our Creator, and we pray for the unification and completion of a world we feel is fragmented.

The words of the Kaddish create a fellowship with others who have suffered loss. It is said in the presence of a public quorum of ten adults (in Hebrew, *minyan*). When a parent dies, one recites Kaddish for eleven months. In theory, mourning for parents continues for twelve months, but traditional Jews consider a full year to be the duration required for judgment of the wicked. Since we do not view our parents as wicked, we demonstrate this by saying Kaddish for eleven months only. Many Jews say it for a full year, retaining the Talmudic custom of mourning. Kaddish is usually recited for a 30-day period for other close relatives - son, daughter, brother, sister and spouse - although sometimes individuals choose to extend the Kaddish period beyond thirty days. Kaddish is also said each year on the anniversary of the death of a loved one (yahrzeit) and at Yizkor services.

Typically, mourners say Kaddish towards the end of the service. In many congregations there is an additional Kaddish for mourners after the Morning Blessings.

Traditionally only the mourners stand during Kaddish. They take three steps back at the last verse, which symbolizes the end of their audience with God, then three steps forward to their original position. In many congregations, *all* the worshipers rise as a sign of respect to the memory of the departed. The entire congregation shows its support and solidarity with the mourners and its remembrance of the victims of the Holocaust who left no one behind to say Kaddish for them.

Reciting the Kaddish in memory of our beloved dead brings us all closer as our voices rhythmically echo all those who have mourned before us. In that moment we form a community which transcends death.

THE MOURNER'S KADDISH

Glorified and hallowed be the great name of God throughout the world which was created according to Divine will.

May the rule of peace be established speedily in our time, unto us and unto the entire household of Israel. Amen.

May God's great name be praised throughout all eternity.

Extolled and glorified, honored and adored, ever be the name of the Holy One. God is beyond the praises and hymns of glory which mortals offer throughout the world. Amen.

May there be a great heavenly peace and life unto us, unto all Israel. Amen.

May the One who ordains the harmony of the universe, bestow peace upon us and upon the whole house of Israel. Amen.

THE MOURNER'S KADDISH

*Yitgadal v'yitkadash sh'mei raba b'alma di v'ra chir'utei,
v'yamlich malchutei b'ḥayeichon u-v'yomeichon u-
v'ḥayei d'chol beit yisrael, ba-agala u-vi-z'man kariv,
v'imru amen.*

Y'hei sh'mei raba m'varach l'alam u-l'almei almaya.

*Yitbarach v'yishtabaḥ v'yitpa'ar v'yitromam v'yitnasei,
v'yit-hadar v'yit'aleh v'yit'halal sh'mei d'kudsha, b'rich hu
l'ela (l'ela mi-kol) min kol birchata v'shirata,
tushb'ḥata v'neḥemata da-amiran b'alma, v'imru amen.*

*Y'hei sh'lama raba min sh'maya v'ḥayim aleinu v'al
kol yisrael, v'imru amen.
Oseh shalom bi-m'romav, hu ya'aseh shalom aleinu v'al
kol yisrael, v'imru amen.*

קַדִּישׁ

יִתְגַּדַּל וְיִתְקַדַּשׁ שְׁמֵהּ רַבָּא בְּעָלְמָא דִי בְרָא
כִרְעוּתֵהּ, וְיַמְלִיךְ מַלְכוּתֵהּ בְּחַיֵּיכוֹן וּבְיוֹמֵיכוֹן,
וּבְחַיֵּי דְכָל בֵּית יִשְׂרָאֵל, בַּעֲגָלָא וּבִזְמַן קָרִיב,
וְאִמְרוּ אָמֵן.

יְהֵא שְׁמֵהּ רַבָּא מְבָרַךְ לְעָלַם וּלְעָלְמֵי עָלְמַיָּא.

יִתְבָּרַךְ וְיִשְׁתַּבַּח, וְיִתְפָּאַר וְיִתְרוֹמַם, וְיִתְנַשֵּׂא
וְיִתְהַדָּר, וְיִתְעַלֶּה וְיִתְהַלָּל שְׁמֵהּ דְקֻדְשָׁא, בְּרִיךְ
הוּא, לְעֵלָּא (לְעֵלָּא) מִן כָּל בִּרְכָתָא וְשִׁירָתָא,
תֻּשְׁבְּחָתָא וְנֶחֱמָתָא, דַּאֲמִירָן בְּעָלְמָא, וְאִמְרוּ
אָמֵן.

יְהֵא שְׁלָמָא רַבָּא מִן שְׁמַיָּא, וְחַיִּים, עָלֵינוּ וְעַל
כָּל יִשְׂרָאֵל, וְאִמְרוּ אָמֵן.

עֹשֶׂה שָׁלוֹם בִּמְרוֹמָיו, הוּא יַעֲשֶׂה שָׁלוֹם עָלֵינוּ
וְעַל כָּל יִשְׂרָאֵל, וְאִמְרוּ אָמֵן.

"God heals the broken-hearted
and binds up their wounds."
Psalm 147:3

WHAT IS SHIVA?

A period of mourning begins immediately after the burial. In Jewish law this mourning process is divided into stages designed to ease the mourner back into the mainstream of life.

Shiva is the initial phase of deepest mourning. It is usually observed for a seven-day period. This intense period of mourning provides an opportunity for the close relatives of the deceased to begin the process of recovery by concentrating on their grief. Relatives who sit shiva are those who have lost a parent, spouse, child or sibling. They remain at home and receive visitors who come to express sympathy and love. The mourners are not left alone; they are surrounded by people who care and share their loss. The visitors also help form a minyan for prayer services in the house of mourning.

Painted Glass Burial Society Cup
Bohemia 1692

The practice of shiva (Hebrew for "seven") probably dates back to Biblical times. When the Patriarch Jacob died, his son Joseph "wailed with a very great and sore wailing, and he made a mourning for his father seven days" (Genesis 50:10). The rabbis of the Talmud specified "three days for weeping and seven for lamenting" (Moed Katan 27b). From this we deduce that the first three days of shiva are the most intense. It is for this reason that some Jews observe shiva for three days only.

Jewish tradition considers a fraction of a day as a complete day. Therefore, the day of burial is considered a full day of mourning, even if the interment takes place late in the afternoon. Similarly, the seventh day is regarded as a full day although mourning is observed for only a short time after sunrise. Shabbat is counted as one of the seven days, but there are no public signs of mourning on this day. On Shabbat, ribbons or torn garments are not worn, and mourners attend synagogue services. The bereaved return to their formal state of mourning at home on Saturday night after Shabbat has ended.

Usually, the shiva period ends on the morning of the seventh day after burial, immediately following the morning prayer service (Shaharit). At that time, the mourners rise from their week of mourning.

The timing and duration of mourning are affected by the holidays of Pesach, Shavuot, Sukkot, Rosh Hashanah and Yom Kippur. The general rule is that these Jewish holidays cancel the shiva. So, for example, if mourning begins on a Wednesday and a Festival starts that night, the remainder of the shiva is nullified. Those few hours of shiva observance are regarded as the equivalent of seven full days. Another example: if someone dies on the first day of Shavuot, the burial takes place on the morning *after* Shavuot. Shiva begins then and lasts for seven days. If, however, the funeral takes place on an intermediate day of a Festival (*Ḥol HaMoed*), the period of shiva does not begin until after the Festival ends. The procedure for holidays that fall during the shiva period can be complicated. It is best to consult your rabbi if this occurs.

"May God comfort you
along with all the mourners
of Zion and Jerusalem."

Greeting to Mourners

HOW IS SHIVA OBSERVED?

SHIVA is observed in the home of the deceased or at a close relative's house.

A special candle is lit upon returning from the cemetery. It burns for the entire shiva period. This shiva candle is commonly provided by the funeral director. In Proverbs 20:27 we read: "The human soul is the light of God." The candlelight symbolizes the soul of the deceased as well as the presence of God. It is a sign of respect to the memory of the deceased.

The mourners eat a *meal of condolence* (in Hebrew, *seudat havra'ah*) when they return from the cemetery. It often includes hard-boiled eggs, the symbol of fertility and

46

life, and bread, the staff of life in Judaism. The meal is usually provided by friends and neighbors. Jewish tradition considers the bringing of food to mourning friends and relatives a mitzvah and an expression of consolation. Throughout the shiva period, it is likely that friends will bring or send platters of food. This helps to free the mourners from some everyday concerns. While it is acceptable to drink wine or liquor at the house of mourning, it should not be for the purpose of merriment or the avoidance of reality.

It is traditional for mirrors to be covered in the house where shiva is observed. This symbolizes withdrawal from worldly concerns when personal appearance becomes unimportant. Many Jews do not cover the mirrors in the house of mourning.

Traditionally, mourners do not sit on chairs of normal height. Instead they sit close to the ground on low stools or benches. This practice may account for the expression "sitting shiva." It is probably based on the Biblical reference to Job, whose three friends came to comfort him and "for seven days and seven nights they sat beside him on the ground" (Job 2:13). The chair need not necessarily be uncomfortable, as long as it is lower than normal. Mourners need not *sit* all the time during shiva. They may stand, walk or lie down to rest. When sitting, the mourner does not rise from his or her chair to greet any visitor, no matter how important that person may be.

An integral part of shiva is the *condolence call*. It is a mitzvah to visit a house of mourning during the shiva period.   In Hebrew this is called *niḥum avelim* or "comforting mourners."   The Talmud teaches that consoling mourners is an act of God (Sotah 14a). One of the first examples of an actual condolence call is when Job's friends "sat with him and none spoke to him for they saw that his suffering was very great" (Job 2:13).

The purpose of the condolence call is to offer companionship to the mourners - to offer support and a sympathetic ear.   Small talk and socializing are discouraged; rather, visitors should speak about the deceased and encourage the mourners to express their feelings.   It is likely that the mourner will experience mood swings; laughter over funny or dear memories may alternate with tears and anger.

Visitors usually do not bring flowers or gifts other than food.   Instead they will often make donations to charity in the name of the deceased.

During the shiva period the mourner does not leave the house and does not work, except if severe financial loss will result.   Some Jews do not wear leather shoes during shiva. These are replaced by canvas or other soft shoes. This is done in a spirit of self-denial and humility, since leather is viewed as a luxury.

Daily prayer services are held in the home of the deceased.   These services take place in the presence of a

Painted Pottery Burial Society Pitcher
Mikulov, Moravia 1836

minyan so that the mourner may recite Kaddish. The services may be held in the morning and/or evening, traditionally for the week of shiva, but sometimes for one or three days. Various changes may be made in the regular prayer service when it is held in a house of mourning. Prayer booklets for this purpose are usually available at the funeral home or from the synagogue. The pattern of services in the home may depend on family tradition or the customs of your synagogue.

When mourners go to the synagogue on the first Shabbat following a loved one's death, they are usually greeted with the words, "May God comfort you along with all the mourners of Zion and Jerusalem."

It is traditional for mourners to end the shiva period by taking a walk around the block to symbolize their return to a more normal life. Some of the prayer booklets intended for a house of mourning include prayers and directions for this brief ritual.

"And God will wipe away tears
from all faces."

Isaiah 25:8

WHAT IS SHELOSHIM?

SHELOSHIM (Hebrew for "thirty")
is a thirty-day period of mourning that begins
immediately after the burial. When Moses died, the
Children of Israel mourned him for thirty days
(Deuteronomy 34:8). Sheloshim includes the shiva period.
Sheloshim constitutes the full period of mourning for all
relatives except parents, who are mourned for eleven or
twelve months. However, some do mourn longer than
thirty days for relatives other than parents.

The period of sheloshim is less restrictive than shiva.
Mourners may return to work but generally do not attend
social gatherings or participate in festive events. Kaddish
is recited daily at the synagogue. Many Jews do not have
haircuts or shave during this period.

Just as in shiva, the observance of sheloshim is affected by the Jewish holidays. It is best to consult your rabbi if a Festival falls during these thirty days.

Those who sat shiva in a community other than their own (for example, where their parent lived) or whose shiva was very brief because of a Festival, may want to hold a minyan at their home to mark the end of sheloshim in order to receive the comfort of their community.

Group Portrait of Members of the Burial Society
Prague ca. 1780

"And Jacob set up a pillar
upon Rachel's grave."

Genesis 35:20

WHAT IS AN UNVEILING?

THE gravestone, or monument, may be erected at the end of shiva or up to twelve months after death. The purpose of the tombstone is to mark the gravesite clearly and permanently.

The monument (in Hebrew, *matzevah*) is usually selected soon after the funeral. The tombstone is simple and can be made of stone or metal. It may lie horizontally or be erected vertically. The inscription on the stone will usually contain a short Hebrew phrase or a Jewish symbol, the Hebrew and English name of the deceased and the Jewish and secular dates of birth and death.

While in many parts of the world there is no formal ceremony of dedication, it is customary in the United States to dedicate the tombstone in a graveside ceremony called an unveiling. The unveiling is the formal removal of a veil or other covering over the tombstone. It symbolizes the official erection of the monument. Immediate family and close friends usually attend the dedication ceremony, which is accompanied by a brief service in memory of the person who has died. The rabbi will usually officiate at this ceremony, although it is not required in Jewish tradition. Several Psalms are recited and a few words are spoken about the deceased. The cloth is removed, the *El Malei Raḥamim* is chanted, and the Kaddish recited.

The unveiling ceremony is often used to mark the end of the mourning period. In any event the occasion should be simple and include only the closest family and friends.

"My help comes from God,
maker of heaven and earth."

Psalm 121:2

WHAT IS YAHRZEIT?

Y AHRZEIT marks the anniversary
of a death. The word is derived from Yiddish and means
"year's time." It is traditionally observed according to the
Hebrew date of death. If a parent dies on the tenth day of
Kislev, 5752, yahrzeit is observed on the tenth day of
Kislev, 5753, and on that Hebrew date every year.
However, some Jews follow the secular calendar.

Most Jews light a yahrzeit candle to commemorate the
day. The candle is lit at sunset on the evening before the
anniversary and is allowed to burn itself out. These
commemorative candles are available in synagogue
giftshops, Judaica stores, supermarkets and in grocery
stores specializing in kosher foods. There are no standard
prayers or prescribed blessings to accompany the lighting
of the candle. One may recite any of the Psalms related to
the funeral service (Psalms 15, 16, 23, 42, 49, 90, 91, 144) or
one's own prayers, readings and reflections. This can be

Yahrzeit Candle

an opportunity to read the Psalms carefully and to choose one or more that are particularly appropriate to your emotions at the time. Special prayers and meditations on lighting a yahrzeit candle are found in many prayerbooks.

On the Shabbat before yahrzeit (or on other days when the Torah is read), the mourner may be called up to the Torah for an aliyah. The aliyah is considered a special honor. Kaddish is recited on the day of yahrzeit or on the Shabbat before yahrzeit. Before Kaddish, the rabbi may read the names of the deceased whose yahrzeit is observed during that week. A bulb will often be lit next to the name of the deceased on the synagogue's memorial plaque.

It is customary to visit the cemetery on or close to this anniversary. Many people perform the mitzvah of giving tzedakah to commemorate the yahrzeit. They may engage in other acts of special kindness at this time.

"There is a time to weep..."

Ecclesiastes 3:4

WHEN IS THE GRAVE VISITED?

JUDAISM discourages frequent grave visitation for it may hinder the mourner's return to normal life. However, there are days when it is traditional to visit the cemetery. These include the days before the High Holy Days, and special personal days like birthdays and anniversaries.

Several blessings and Psalms may be recited at the graveside, including the memorial prayer, *El Malei Rahamim.*

Visitors to the grave often leave a small stone on the tombstone as a symbol of the enduring bond between the visitor and the deceased. It is an act of love, a gesture to show that you were there.

PSALM 121

I lift my eyes to the mountains;
What is the source of my help?
My help comes from Adonai,
Maker of heaven and earth.

God will not let your foot give way;
your Protector will not slumber.
See, the Protector of Israel
neither slumbers nor sleeps!

God is your Guardian,
God is your protection
at your right hand.
The sun will not strike you by day,
nor the moon by night.

God will guard you from all harm
God will guard your soul,
your going and coming,
now and forever.

"May the souls be bound up
in the bond of life
with the souls of all the righteous."
from the Yizkor service

WHAT IS YIZKOR?

A memorial service called Yizkor (Hebrew for "may God remember") is held in the synagogue on major Jewish holidays: Yom Kippur, Shemini Atzeret and the last days of Pesach and Shavuot. Yizkor usually takes place in the morning after the Torah service. Many Jews light a memorial candle on the eve of days on which Yizkor is said.

It is believed that Yizkor was introduced into the worship services during the massacres of the Christian Crusades and medieval pogroms (twelfth century). A memorial service was introduced on Yom Kippur to honor those Jews who were killed. Subsequently, Yizkor became a service to remember Jewish martyrs and our own deceased loved ones as well. During the eighteenth century Yizkor came to be recited four times a year, rather than once on Yom Kippur.

Yizkor is recited beginning on the first holiday after the death. Some congregants leave the synagogue during Yizkor if their parents are living. This is *not* a requirement in Jewish practice. In synagogues where the congregants remain throughout, Kaddish may be recited for friends or relatives who have died, or in memory of Jewish martyrs.

"Yizkor" is the first word of the Memorial Prayer (*Hazkarat Neshamot*). One prayer may be said for all one's deceased, naming each person in the blank spaces indicated. Or, an individual prayer may be recited for each one. *El Malei Raḥamim*, Kaddish and other prayers may also be recited.

Yizkor is an opportunity for making contributions in the name of the deceased to perpetuate their memories and to promote the values they held.

YIZKOR PRAYER

IN REMEMBRANCE OF A FATHER:

יִזְכֹּר אֱלֹהִים נִשְׁמַת אָבִי מוֹרִי.... שֶׁהָלַךְ לְעוֹלָמוֹ. בַּעֲבוּר
שֶׁאֲנִי נוֹדֵר צְדָקָה בַּעֲדוֹ, בִּשְׂכַר זֶה, תְּהֵא נַפְשׁוֹ צְרוּרָה
בִּצְרוֹר הַחַיִּים עִם נִשְׁמוֹת אַבְרָהָם יִצְחָק וְיַעֲקֹב, שָׂרָה
רִבְקָה רָחֵל וְלֵאָה, וְעִם שְׁאָר צַדִּיקִים וְצִדְקָנִיּוֹת שֶׁבְּגַן
עֵדֶן. אָמֵן.

May God remember the soul of my revered father .... who has
gone to his eternal rest. In remembrance of him, I shall perform acts of
charity and goodness. May his soul be bound up in the bond of
eternal life, in the company of the immortal souls of Abraham, Isaac
and Jacob, of Sarah, Rebecca, Rachel and Leah, and of all the righteous,
who have merited the bliss of immortality. Amen.

IN REMEMBRANCE OF A MOTHER:

יִזְכּוֹר אֱלֹהִים נִשְׁמַת אִמִּי מוֹרָתִי.... שֶׁהָלְכָה לְעוֹלָמָהּ.
בַּעֲבוּר שֶׁאֲנִי נוֹדֵר צְדָקָה בַּעֲדָהּ, בִּשְׂכַר זֶה, תְּהֵא נַפְשָׁהּ
צְרוּרָה בִּצְרוֹר הַחַיִּים עִם נִשְׁמוֹת אַבְרָהָם יִצְחָק וְיַעֲקֹב,
שָׂרָה רִבְקָה רָחֵל וְלֵאָה, וְעִם שְׁאָר צַדִּיקִים וְצִדְקָנִיּוֹת
שֶׁבְּגַן עֵדֶן. אָמֵן.

May God remember the soul of my revered mother .... who has
gone to her eternal rest. In remembrance of her, I shall perform acts of
charity and goodness. May her soul be bound up in the bond of
eternal life, in the company of the immortal souls of Abraham, Isaac
and Jacob, of Sarah, Rebecca, Rachel and Leah, and of all the righteous,
who have merited the bliss of immortality. Amen.

"May God give strength to our people.

May God bless our people with peace."

Psalm 29:11